A Beginner's GUIDE to ELeCTRiCiTY aND MAGNeTism

Gill Arbuthnott

CONSULTANT NICK ARMSTRONG

ILLUSTRATED BY Marc Mones

A & C BLACK

To Barbara, the light of Nick's life (even though
she struggles to understand electricity and magnetism)

First published 2016 by
A & C Black, an imprint of Bloomsbury Publishing Plc
50 Bedford Square, London, WC1B 3DP

www.bloomsbury.com

Bloomsbury is a registered trademark of Bloomsbury Publishing Plc

Additional images all Shutterstock, aside from the following: P17 Ambroise Tardieu/
Wikimedia Commons, p19 Manuel Muñoz, p22 Wellcome Trust/Wikimedia Commons,
p25 Imperial War Museum/Wikimedia Commons, p58 "Promptuarii Iconum Insigniorum"/
Wikimedia Commons, p58 Popular Science Monthly Volume 59/Wikimedia Commons,
p58 The Life of James Clerk Maxwell/Wikimedia Commons, p59 Wikimedia Commons.

ISBN 978-1-4729-1574-0

A CIP catalogue for this book is available from the British Library.

Printed in China by Leo Paper Products, Heshan, Guangdong

1 3 5 7 9 10 8 6 4 2

Contents

Introduction

Try to imagine a world without electricity… No phone, no games console, no laptop. You could get by without these if you had to (yes, really!), but how about no light, no heat, no way to cook? We take electricity for granted, but we'd be lost without it, and we've only known how to generate and safely use it for less than 150 years.

You probably don't know very much about what electricity really is. And I bet you don't know how closely electricity and magnetism are linked. This book will take you through the fascinating story of how we learned to understand and harness electricity and magnetism. Want to know why a compass works, which horror story was inspired by an experiment on frogs, and what the connection is between static electricity and dinosaurs?

Then read on!

The Mighty Atom

You can't really get to grips with electricity and magnetism until you understand what atoms are, so that's where we'll start. And we're not starting with a scientist, but with a philosopher (someone who spends their time sitting around and thinking).

This was an ancient Greek philosopher called Democritus. He started thinking about what would happen if you took something like a piece of gold and cut it in half, then cut it in half again, and kept on doing that. Would you just get smaller and smaller bits of gold, or would you reach a point when it was so small that you couldn't cut it in half any more? Democritus called this tiny, uncuttable thing atomos, and today we call it an atom.

Democritus was a philosopher from ancient Greece.

Gold

However, Democritus wasn't quite right about his theory, because atoms are made of smaller particles, but if you 'cut up' an atom of gold, it isn't gold any more. So an atom is the smallest particle of a chemical element.

Empty space

Atoms are much too small to see, even with the most powerful microscope, so scientists have had to work out what they are like from the results of experiments. And guess what? Most of an atom is empty space! This is very hard to imagine (just try imagining emptiness).

But this idea might help: if the whole atom was the size of a small island, the only thing in it would be a nucleus the size of a coconut in the middle, and electrons like tiny mosquitoes flying round the edge. The rest is just…nothing!

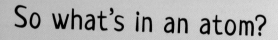

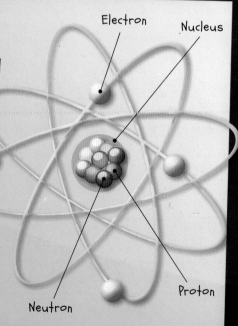

So what's in an atom?

The nucleus is made up of particles called protons and neutrons and contains almost all the mass of the atom. Protons have a positive charge, and neutrons have no charge. Whizzing round the nucleus are electrons — particles so tiny that they have virtually no mass at all. They do have a negative charge though. This means that the positive charges on the protons are perfectly balanced by the negative charges on the electrons.

Electron

Nucleus

Neutron

Proton

Static Electricity

Now we know a bit about atoms we can look at some of the early discoveries about electricity over the next few pages. Back to ancient Greece first!

Amber

If you look at a pine tree, you might see sticky areas on the bark. Or, if you look at freshly cut pine wood, sometimes you can find a sticky yellowish substance leaking out. This is called resin and when it hardens it is known as amber. The Greek word for amber is ἠλεκτρον (electron), which means something like 'the beaming sun'. Amber can be polished to make beautiful honey-coloured stones, which are used to make jewellery. The ancient Greeks were the first to use it like this, but they also discovered that if you rubbed it with fur, it could pick up little bits of dry straw. Although they didn't know it at the time, they had just discovered static electricity.

Resin from the bark of a pine tree.

Try it yourself

If you know someone with some amber jewellery, offer to polish it for them, and see if you can get it to pick up tiny bits of paper (make sure they say yes before you start the experiment!).

Don't worry if you don't know anyone with amber jewellery, you can try the same thing with a plastic ruler instead. Rub it hard for about twenty seconds with a wool or cotton jumper and the little bits of paper should stick to the ruler. Don't give up if it doesn't work the first time — it can be a bit temperamental.

Amber and science fiction

Insects sometimes become trapped in sticky plant resin. They won't rot when they die if they are completely covered by the resin. And if the resin hardens into amber, they become preserved in it. This has been happening for millions of years, and scientists have been able to study insect species that have been extinct for centuries by looking at specimens preserved in amber.

The author Michael Crichton used this idea in his book *Jurassic Park*. His scientists found blood-sucking insects from the age of the dinosaurs preserved in amber, and were able to extract dinosaur blood cells from them. They extracted the dinosaur DNA (the chemical instructions for building a dinosaur) and used it to recreate dinosaurs for their new theme park. It's highly unlikely we'll ever be able to recreate dinosaurs like this however, as you can't get complete dinosaur DNA from the insects.

Electric and Magnetic Charges

Hundreds of years ago scientists had to try and explain static electricity and the idea of charge without knowing anything at all about protons and electrons. Here are some of those early ideas, which introduced terms we still use today to describe electricity and magnetism.

Electric charges

Electric charges can attract or repel each other. But why does this happen? A scientist called Benjamin Franklin came up with the idea that there are two electrical charges, and called them positive and negative. Positive attracts negative, but positive repels positive and negative repels negative.

What is charge? Well, no one really knows – not even scientists like Einstein or Stephen Hawking! Charge is a 'concept' – an idea that explains how protons and electrons behave.

Magnetic charges

Magnets attract and repel too. Because the word charges has already been used for electricity, we say that magnets have two poles. We call these the North and South poles. Just like electric charges, North attracts South, but North repels North and South repels South.

Magnetic electrons!

Moving electric charges produce magnetic fields. In atoms, the electrons are whizzing around the nucleus in circles, producing magnetic fields as they do so. However, some electrons are moving clockwise and others are moving anticlockwise, and this makes them produce magnetic fields that cancel each other out, so the whole atom doesn't have a magnetic field we can detect. If all the electrons moved in the same direction, they would produce a magnetic field.

Lightning

Lightning is a very powerful discharge of static electricity (see page 8). Many lightning flashes are over five kilometres high! They usually start in huge cumulonimbus storm clouds. Some lightning flashes go from one cloud to another, but we are more aware of the ones that hit the ground. They do this if the cloud and the ground under it have opposite charges, creating an electric field.

If lightning hits a tree, it can make the trunk explode as the sap inside is vaporised, and if it hits sand, it can make it so hot that some of the sand turns into a glass-like substance. There are about 100 lightning strikes every second, worldwide. The village of Kifuka in the Democratic Republic of Congo has the most and gets about 158 strikes per square kilometre every year.

Benjamin Franklin and the storm kite

Benjamin Franklin led a very busy life. He was an author, politician, postmaster, diplomat, scientist and inventor (phew!). Among his many inventions were bifocal glasses and the lightning rod.

He famously designed a very dangerous experiment to show that lightning is electricity, by flying a kite into a storm. **Never ever** fly a kite in stormy weather, as it can be **extremely** dangerous and people have been killed doing this.

People who tried Franklin's experiment were able to extract sparks from thunderclouds. It was through this experiment that Franklin realised that he had found a way to protect buildings from lightning strikes. By attaching a pointed metal rod to the roof, and running a wire from this down the outside of the building all the way to the ground, Franklin discovered that the lightning rod would attract the lightning more effectively than the rest of the building, and the electric charge would run harmlessly down the wire and into the ground.

From Frogs to Frankenstein

A scientist called Luigi Galvani began to experiment on frog muscles in the 1790s. He found that if the nerve in a dead frog's leg was touched with a piece of charged metal, its leg would twitch as the muscles contracted. He called this effect 'animal electricity' and it later became known as Galvanism. He thought at the time that animals had some sort of electric fluid flowing through their bodies. However, later work proved he was wrong.

Amazing electric cows!

The public were fascinated by Galvani's findings, and even more so by the work of his nephew, Giovanni Aldini. He put charged wires into the heads of dead cows and found that he could make their mouths open and close and their tongues stick out.

Frankenstein

A young novelist called Mary Godwin had read about these experiments when she was on holiday in Switzerland with the writers Percy Shelley, Lord Byron and John Polidori. They had a competition to see who could write the best horror story. Mary remembered reading about Galvanism and the attempts to reanimate dead bodies, and this was one of the ideas that she used in her famous novel Frankenstein. (She later married Percy Shelley and is better known as Mary Shelley.)

John Polidori used the story that Byron wrote that night as the basis for his novel *The Vampyre* – the first ever vampire novel. What a night!

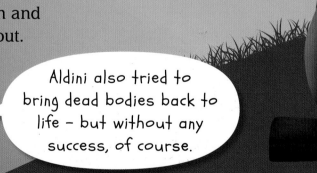

Aldini also tried to bring dead bodies back to life – but without any success, of course.

The first battery

Alessandro Volta noticed that in Galvani's 'twitching frog' experiments, the frog's leg had two different metals in contact with the nerve to make the muscle twitch.

Volta tried a range of metals, and found that Zinc and Copper worked best to make the muscle move. Volta used his discoveries to make the first battery, from discs of Zinc and Copper separated by paper soaked in salty water. Volta's work is really the start of what we think of as electricity. Other scientists used Volta's battery to do experiments with a flow of electric charge – an electric current. This could be easily controlled, unlike static electricity, which we met earlier in the book.

You can try a version of the 'twitching frog' experiment yourself – but by using a lemon instead of a frog! You'll find instructions on page 55. Remember to ask an adult's permission before getting started.

Alessandro Volta.

Simple Electric Circuits

Over the next few pages, we're going to be talking about what happens in electric circuits. Let's begin by looking at a simple one – the sort you might find in a torch, for example. Although this is a simple circuit, the ideas that we will discover are true for any electrical system.

The word circuit just means something that starts and finishes in the same place, like a Formula One race circuit. Electricity can only flow if there is a complete circuit for it to travel round. In an electrical circuit the 'road' must be made from materials that conduct electricity. In a simple circuit these are wires. We'll come back to the idea of complete circuits several times, especially on pages 38-39.

Let's look at a torch as an example. As soon as the switch is closed the electrons, which carry electrical charge and energy, start moving, and the lamp lights up. But here's the puzzle: electrons move more slowly than snails!

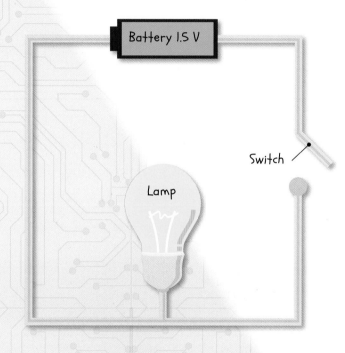

Battery 1.5 V

Switch

Lamp

If the wire between the battery and the lamp was ten centimetres long it would take an electron about three minutes to get from one to the other, so how can the lamp light up so quickly? It's the same when you switch on a ceiling light at home. The switch on the wall is probably several metres away from the bulb, but when you press the switch, the light comes on instantly. So what's happening?

Pushing

It's because instead of each electron having to whizz – or we should say crawl – all the way from the battery to the lamp, it just gives its neighbour a push, then that gives the next electron a push and so on…so it's really the push that is moving, not the electrons. When the switch is closed, the battery pushes electron one forward. Electron one repels electron two, giving it a tiny push, electron two does the same to electron three and so on. Electron seven in the diagram pushes electron eight into the lamp, making it light up, and eleven pushes twelve into the battery – making it a full circuit.

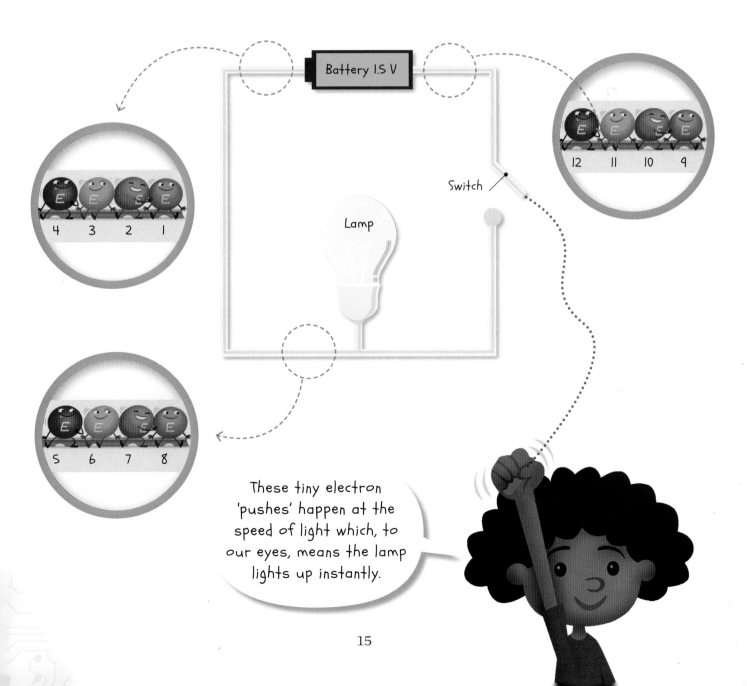

Battery 1.5 V

12 11 10 9

Switch

4 3 2 1

Lamp

5 6 7 8

These tiny electron 'pushes' happen at the speed of light which, to our eyes, means the lamp lights up instantly.

The Volt

This was named after Alessandro Volta (see page 13). It is a unit of measurement in electricity. It tells us how much energy an electric charge has. You sometimes hear people saying things like, "The number of volts running through the circuit is..." This doesn't actually make sense! It's like saying, "The height running through the mountain is 1000 metres." Heights don't run, and neither do volts. There is no Usain Volt!

Volta

What is a volt?

So what is a volt? Imagine you are in a building with stairs and a lift. You carry a tennis ball up one floor in the lift, and let it roll back to ground level down the stairs. A battery is like the lift – it's a way of giving energy to something. In the building this is the ball – in electrical terms it's an electron.

The ball rolling down the stairs is losing energy. In our circuit the equivalent is the electrons losing their energy to power a bulb. The voltage is equivalent to the height you take the ball up in the lift – more height is equivalent to greater voltage. And the distance the ball goes up in the lift must be the same as the distance it comes down by the stairs.

What is an Amp?

No, not an amplifier for your electric guitar! An Amp, or Ampere to give it its full name, is the unit we use to measure electric current (how much charge is flowing around a circuit).

You might have heard of Hans Christian Anderson, who wrote fairy stories.

He had a friend called Hans Christian Oersted (that must have been confusing) who was a scientist and who found that an electric current would make a compass needle move. This meant it must be creating a magnetic field.

André Marie Ampère.

French scientist André Marie Ampère was very interested in this, and wanted to know more about how magnetic fields and electricity are related. He spent a long time doing some very complicated maths to work out how strong the magnetic field is around a wire that has an electric current flowing through it. The Amp is named after him.

Magnetic Elements

All atoms produce magnetic fields, but not many elements are magnetic. (Elements are pure substances that contain a single type of atom.)

In magnetic elements the atoms clump together and the electrons move around them in a sort of Mexican wave. This gives the group of atoms a magnetic field. Iron is the best-known magnetic element. In a non-magnetic lump of iron, the magnetic fields produced by the atoms point in random directions and cancel each other out.

However in an iron magnet, the magnetic fields produced by the atoms all point in the same direction. (Turn to page 54 for instructions on how to make your own magnet.) Elements with the same type of magnetic fields as iron are called ferromagnetic materials (this is from the Latin word for iron, which is ferrum) – and there aren't many of them. Nickel and Cobalt are ferromagnetic, and so are some more exotic metals like Gadolinium and Neodymium.

Try it Yourself

Sometimes you might find coins down the back of the sofa. Impress your friends by telling them how old the coins are without looking at the date on them!

One and two pence coins used to be made of an alloy of copper called bronze. (An alloy is a mixture of two elements, at least one of which must be a metal.)

Since 1992 however, they have been made out of copper plated steel. Steel contains lots of iron, so you can separate the new ones from the old ones with a magnet. (You'll only find non-magnetic ones if they've been down the sofa for a long time though!)

There was an exception to this rule in 1998 when 2 pence coins were produced in both alloys.

2 pence coin from 1992.

2 pence coin from 1998.

2 pence coin from 2015.

The Earth's Magnetic Field

The Earth's core contains lots of iron. The very centre of the Earth is a solid ball of metals and a thick layer of molten iron and nickel surrounds it.

These two layers are very, very hot – probably about as hot as the surface of the sun (that's about 6000 degrees Centigrade), but the bit in the middle stays solid because of the enormous pressure it's under. The liquid part of the core all rotates around the solid bit in the same direction. This is like a giant version of what happens in an atom – electrons rotating around a nucleus – and so it produces a giant magnetic field.

Magnetic field

Crust

Mantle

Outer core

Inner core

I always wondered what was really at the centre of the earth.

10

There are two north poles...

Amaze your friends with this strange fact – the magnetic North Pole and the geographic North Pole aren't in the same place! They aren't always the same distance apart either, because the magnetic North Pole wobbles around by as much as ten miles a year as the Earth's magnetic field changes. It does this because the molten swirling part of the core has currents, just like the oceans, and these change from time to time.

You must be flipping joking!

Geophysicists know from looking at ancient lava samples that the Earth's magnetic field 'flips' every so often – the North Pole becomes the South Pole and vice versa. This happens about once every 500,000 years, and it looks as if the next flip is due soon. Well, soonish. Within the next few thousand years anyway! Would this matter? It would certainly be confusing for animals that navigate using the magnetic field, but would it affect us?

The Earth's magnetic field is getting gradually weaker – something that scientists believe happens in the run-up to a flip. Since the magnetic field usually protects Earth from cosmic radiation (dangerous radiation from space) we could be affected, with power and communication systems most likely to be damaged. Don't worry though, we probably have a few hundred years to prepare for it happening.

Compasses

The first compasses were invented in China about 2,000 years ago. However, they weren't used for finding which direction to travel in, but for fortune telling and Feng Shui – a way of deciding the best and luckiest place to build houses.

The first compasses were made from lodestone, a naturally magnetic iron ore. A piece hanging from a thread would always turn to point the same way – it was lining up with the Earth's magnetic field. In later compasses, magnetised iron needles replaced the lodestone.

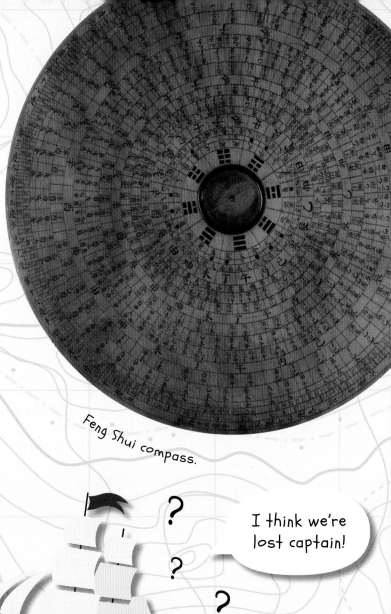

Feng Shui compass.

I think we're lost captain!

Before compasses were available, it was very dangerous to sail out of sight of land – you could change direction without realising, and you might never find your way home again!

Compass confusion!

Take a deep breath and we'll get through this next bit together...
We worked out that the Earth has a magnetic field, so if it's basically a magnet, it must have a North and South pole. It's obvious where they will be – at the North and South poles. Absolutely right, but the magnetic North pole is at the geographic South pole and the magnetic South pole is at the geographical North pole.

Don't panic! Here's the explanation.

The geographic North pole is the direction in which the North end of a bar magnet points if you suspend it from a string...so if the North pole of a magnet is attracted to it, it must be a south pole. Remember what we discovered on page 7: North attracts South, North repels North and South repels South.

A compass needle is a tiny bar magnet arranged so it can spin inside the compass and point along the Earth's magnetic field. The North pole of the compass needle is attracted to the South pole of the Earth's magnetic field. Right. Off you go and have a lie down now so your brain can recover.

Magnetic South Pole

Geographic North Pole

S

N

Geographic South Pole

Magnetic North Pole

What the Earth's Magnetic Field Does

We are very lucky that the Earth has a magnetic field. The sun is like a giant hydrogen bomb and is constantly hurling huge quantities of radioactive particles at us. The magnetic field acts like a shield and deflects these particles away from the Earth's surface and towards the poles.

Aurora borealis.

The Northern Lights

You can see this in action if you are lucky enough to see the Northern Lights (or the Southern Lights in Australia and New Zealand).

The aurora borealis, as it is also known, is caused by these particles interacting with oxygen in the atmosphere and being pulled around by the magnetic field. It appears as beautiful wavering curtains of green, purple or red light.

The best places to see the Northern Lights are in Iceland, Greenland and Scandinavia, but during some winters you can see them from parts of the United Kingdom.

Animal magnetism

Homing pigeons are released many miles from their homes and can find their way back home. But how do they find their way? They can't read maps, they don't have Sat Nav and they might be flying from somewhere they've never been, so they can't use landmarks to help them along their way.

The reason they can find their way is because they are using the Earth's magnetic field to navigate. We now know that pigeons (and many other birds) have magnetic particles in their skulls, which lets them detect the magnetic field – something humans can't do.

Homing pigeons from WWII.

Homing pigeons

Homing pigeons have been used for hundreds of years to deliver messages and send news. They were an important method of communication during World War II, and some of them were awarded the Dickin Medal – the animal equivalent of the Victoria Cross for bravery.

Scientists are now finding more and more types of animal with this 'extra' sense, called magnetoreception. It has been found in bacteria, fruit flies, salamanders and turtles. No one understands exactly how it works yet.

What do Magnets do For Us?

Ooh… Loads of things! For a start, have a look at your fridge door. It will have a rubber seal around it. Inside the seal is a magnet, which is attracted to the fridge, because the metal in it contains a lot of iron. This allows the door to be tightly sealed when you shut it, and prevents heat from the kitchen warming up food in the fridge.

MRI scanners

In hospitals, doctors sometimes use an MRI scanner. This is a Magnetic Resonance Image scanner. The patient lies down in a tube which has a big coil of wire around it. This coil produces a huge magnetic field, which alters the way electrons spin in atoms. Radio signals can detect this change and use it to build up a picture of the organs inside the patient, so a doctor can see if something is wrong without having to carry out an operation.

It sounds a bit dangerous, but it's very safe, and doesn't hurt at all (though you do have to lie very still for quite a while). You can't wear any jewellery in the scanner. If it contains any iron, the magnet pulls it off, and if it's made of gold it gets very hot. For the same reason, you can't have an MRI scan if you have, for example, a metal hip or a pacemaker. It's also incredibly noisy. It's like lying with your head in a hole in the road while someone is using a road drill just beside you!

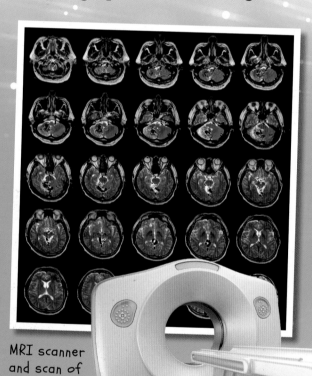

MRI scanner and scan of a brain.

The biggest experiment in the world

Just outside Geneva in Switzerland is CERN. It has a 27 kilometre long, ring-shaped tunnel, 100 metres underground. It would take a top Olympic athlete about 90 minutes to run around it!

The letters CERN stand for the French words for European Organisation for Nuclear Research.

CERN laboratory in Geneva, Switzerland.

This tunnel has 6000 magnets, each stronger than the one in an MRI scanner, to steer particles round the tunnel at high speed. In 2012 the CERN particle accelerator became famous for detecting a particle called the Higgs Boson. It took the two biggest magnets in the world, each the size of St Paul's cathedral, to detect the Higgs Boson!

St Paul's cathedral, London.

27

Electricity from Magnets

Ampere

Oersted

Michael Faraday.

Scientists are always building on each other's work. Michael Faraday knew that Oersted and Ampere (page 17) had shown that an electric current could produce a magnetic field. Aha! thought Faraday. But does it work the other way round? Will a magnetic field produce an electric current?

Faraday's discovery

Faraday found that a coil of wire wrapped around a magnet will produce a current, but only if one moves and the other doesn't – for instance if the magnet moves inside the coil of wire. You can watch this happen in some torches, which have a magnet and a coil of wire in the handle.

To make them work, you just shake them and the bulb lights up. Even when you stop shaking, the bulb stays on for a while. This is because the torch also contains a device called a capacitor, which can store electrical energy. Its ability to store energy is measured in Farads – named after Faraday.

Once Faraday had made his discovery, people quickly designed devices called generators. These are machines that use rotation as the form of movement to produce an electric current. They either rotate a magnet in a coil of wire or a coil of wire in a magnet. It makes no difference which way you do it!

Good grief — I've invented the motor!

Faraday had another, *Aha!* moment. If movement between a magnet and a coil of wire produces electricity, could electricity produce movement? The answer was yes! Faraday had just invented the electric motor. His wasn't very good, but he had to leave something for the other scientists to discover.

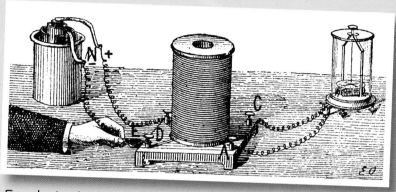

Faraday's electromagnetic motor.

Now we use electric motors everywhere. If you set a mobile phone to vibrate, it's using an electric motor. So is the fan that stops a laptop overheating, and the motor that makes the hard disk rotate. And of course, electric cars have electric motors instead of petrol-driven ones. Then there are games consoles, washing machines, hairdryers, food mixers... The list goes on and on.

I wonder how many electric motors are in your house?

Let There Be Light!

Electricity is basically useless. Ha! You weren't expecting that, were you? But it's true. Electricity itself only does one useful thing for us. Everything else we think of as being 'electricity' isn't; it's electricity that's been changed into something that is actually useful like heat, light, sound or movement.

So what's the one useful thing electricity does?

Electricity is the easiest and quickest way we have of getting energy from one place to another, and that, of course, is vital.

Who invented the lightbulb?

Most people who think they know the answer to this question will say Thomas Edison. You can tell them they're wrong! It was actually a British pharmacist (that's the old word for chemist) called Joseph Swan. Swan's bulbs weren't very good, but they were good enough to light his house and the Savoy Theatre in London, which was the first public building in Britain to have electric light. When Swan gave his friend, Lord Armstrong, bulbs to light his huge house, Armstrong wasn't impressed, because the light was very dim. He realised this was because the generator he had wasn't producing enough electrical energy, so what did he do? He redesigned it. He later bought Bamburgh castle in Northumberland and spent a fortune restoring it. You can see one of his generators there.

Joseph Swan.

Thomas Edison.

What did Edison do?

What Edison did was modify Swan's design and make a better bulb. Many people still use this type of bulb today. It has a very thin wire inside, and when an electric current is passed through it, it gets very hot. It reaches 2000 degrees Celsius, and the wire becomes white-hot and produces light.

Edison's lightbulb from 1882.

Which Lightbulb?

There are several different types of lightbulb available at the moment. Which ones do you use in your house?

Incandescent bulbs

These were developed by Swan and Edison (see pages 31 and 34). Inside the glass bulb is a coil of thin tungsten wire and an inert gas (one that doesn't react with the wire). When a current passes through the wire it gets so hot that it glows and gives off light. However it's very inefficient, which is why we are being encouraged not to use them any more. Only about 5% of the energy these bulbs use is turned into light. The rest is changed into heat. Halogen bulbs work in a very similar way.

Low energy bulbs and fluorescent tube bulbs

These are the same thing – just made in different shapes. Electrons on mercury atoms inside the bulb are given enough energy to give out ultraviolet light. This is invisible to us, but it hits a special coating on the inside of the bulb and is converted to visible light. These bulbs use less than one third of the energy of an incandescent bulb, and last for years, but they can take up to a minute to reach full brightness and the mercury they contain is toxic.

LED bulbs

These tiny bulbs are increasingly being used in torches, and now are starting to be used as replacements for low energy bulbs in household lights. LED stands for light-emitting diode. This is a semi-conductor (these are explained on page 50) that emits light when electrons move around within it. They use even less energy than low energy bulbs, and can last for up to twenty years! The scientists who invented these bulbs were awarded a Nobel Prize in 2014.

DC and AC: The War of the Currents

No, not the sort you put in cakes – those are currants! These are electric currents, and there are two sorts, called DC and AC.

Once electric lighting was invented, a supply of electricity was needed. Thomas Edison designed and built DC generators, and although they were inefficient they were good enough to be used to give New York City its first electric lights.

Direct Current

DC stands for Direct Current. This is the sort of current you get from batteries. The battery pushes the current around the circuit. The voltage in the circuit is not very large, which should make it reasonably safe, but it's not very efficient because the wires heat up. If you try to send electricity far away like this most of the energy gets lost as heat and hardly any electrical energy is left. So a bulb would be dimmer the further from the source it was.

Alternating Current

Living in New York at that time was another scientist called Nikola Tesla. He thought that AC would be much more efficient, so he started to build generators that produced AC currents. AC stands for Alternating Current. This is where the generator pushes and pulls the electrons. You can find out why it's more efficient on pages 38-39.

Angry Edison

Edison was furious, when he heard about the AC currents. If AC was used, he wouldn't be making money from his DC generators! He tried to persuade politicians in New York that AC was too dangerous to use. He even killed stray animals with AC to demonstrate this! He did lots of other dangerous things to try and persuade people to use his DC current. (One idea even led to the invention of the electric chair.)

Tesla comes out on top

Despite Edison's complaints, Tesla's system was much more efficient, and the AC system was adopted. The high voltage involved is why mains electricity is dangerous and you must **never** experiment with it. Tesla's name lives on even today – the Tesla is now used as a unit for measuring magnetic fields.

Thomas Edison

Nikola Tesla

Generating Electricity in Power Stations

To make the steam we need heat... and this is the difficult bit.

We have already mentioned that generators work by rotating a magnet inside a coil of wire or a coil of wire inside a magnet, but what makes it rotate? In most power stations a fan is connected to the bit that is going to rotate, and high-pressure steam is blasted at the fan to make it rotate.

A nuclear power station and wind generators can be used to make power but both have their downsides.

Making steam

We can get the heat by burning coal, oil or gas, but this produces greenhouse gases. Or we can use uranium to generate nuclear power, but this leaves behind dangerous waste. Wind generators don't need steam, so they don't produce waste that harms the environment, but you don't get any electricity if it's not windy – or if it's too windy.

Water works too!

We can use flowing water, but the water needs to be stored high up mountains so that it can generate the energy it needs to turn a turbine (a type of water wheel) as it runs downhill. This is a good way to generate electricity if you live somewhere hilly like Scotland, but not if you live somewhere flat like Holland! Scientists are trying to develop ways to use waves in the sea or tidal flow, but it isn't reliable enough yet.

Hydroelectric power station.

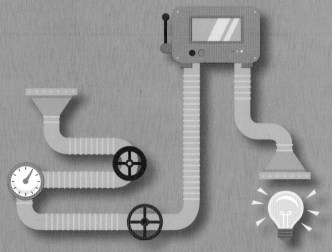

You only get out what you put in

We can't get electrical energy from nothing – we must use another form of energy such as movement and turn it into electrical energy. And the more electrical energy we want to take out, the more energy from another source we have to put in.

Distributing Electricity

The electricity generated in power stations is at dangerously high voltages and this is why it is carried by two wires positioned high above the ground. When it gets to where it will be used, it is transformed back to a low voltage and high current to make it safer.

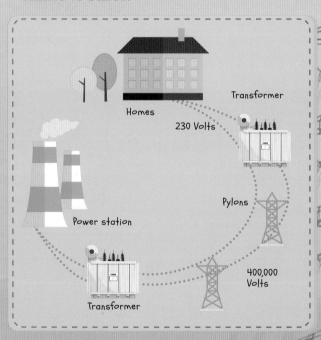

Homes

Transformer

230 Volts

Pylons

Power station

400,000 Volts

Transformer

This may look complicated, but it is really just a huge version of a simple circuit like the one in a torch (see page 14).

There will be a transformer somewhere near your house. Don't **ever** go near it – it's a dangerous device.

What's going on in that wall?

If the sockets in your house have three holes in them then the following is what is happening in them:

• Behind the hole on the right is the wire going back to the power station. You need this to make a complete circuit or the electricity won't flow.

• The hole at the top is a safety device and normally doesn't conduct electricity.

• Behind the hole on the left is the wire coming from the power station.

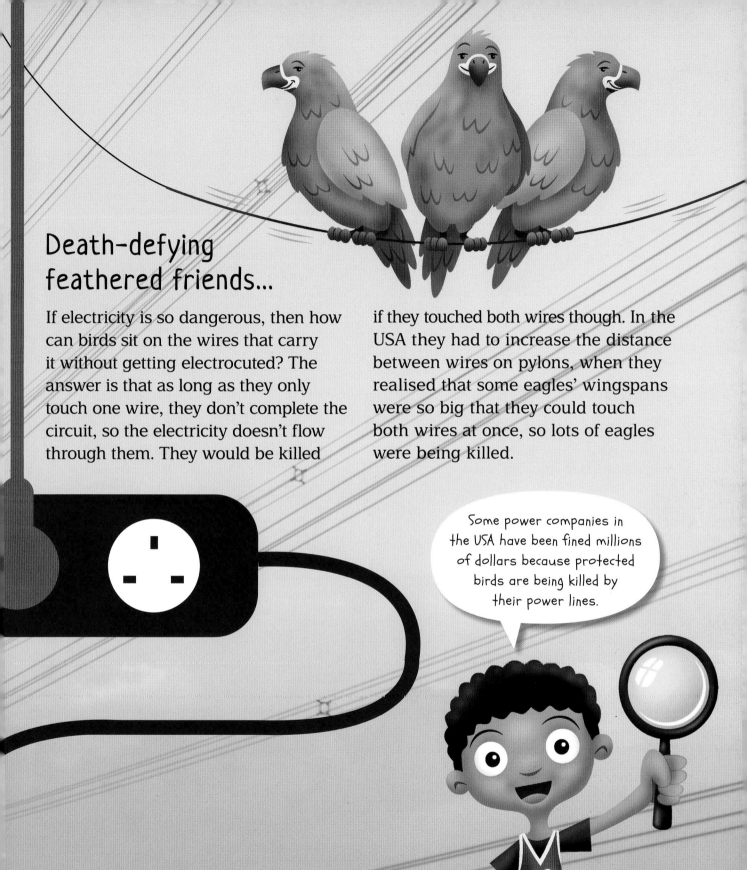

Death-defying feathered friends...

If electricity is so dangerous, then how can birds sit on the wires that carry it without getting electrocuted? The answer is that as long as they only touch one wire, they don't complete the circuit, so the electricity doesn't flow through them. They would be killed if they touched both wires though. In the USA they had to increase the distance between wires on pylons, when they realised that some eagles' wingspans were so big that they could touch both wires at once, so lots of eagles were being killed.

Some power companies in the USA have been fined millions of dollars because protected birds are being killed by their power lines.

Electric Animals

Animals can certainly be killed by electricity, but Galvani thought there was a special sort of electricity in living things that was different from 'normal' electricity (see page 12). He was wrong about it being different, but he was right about electricity existing in animals. Many animals have a nervous system, and the signals it carries are electrical impulses. The energies involved are absolutely tiny though – they are measured in millivolts (thousandths of a volt). Compare this to the electricity supply in your house, which is 230 volts.

Electric eels

Electric eels live in South America, in muddy fresh water. They use electricity for hunting, defence, and communicating with other eels. They produce electricity from special organs that fill 80% of their body, and act like a living battery to produce up to 650 volts. The electricity is only produced for a fraction of a second, which means it would be unlikely to kill you, even if you touched one.

It's probably best not to test this though!

More amazing electric animals

Other animals that can generate their own electricity include catfish, electric rays and some deep-sea microbes. Some scientists think that the yellow stripes on the bodies of oriental hornets act like tiny solar cells and generate electricity!

Varying voltage

The eels can alter the voltage they produce, depending on what it's for. They use a small charge (under ten volts) to navigate and locate their prey, and a much higher voltage to hunt. It's not entirely clear why they don't give themselves shocks. One theory is that because the electric pulse lasts for such a short time and the eels are such large animals, it doesn't have much effect on them, but it will stun smaller fish nearby.

Electric ray.

Fossil Fuels

Until recently, all of our electricity was generated by burning fossil fuels. But what exactly are fossil fuels? Fossil fuels are coal, gas and oil. They are the fossilised remains of animals and plants that lived millions of years ago.

Oil and gas

Oil and gas are formed from the remains of tiny, one-celled plants and animals that lived in lakes and seas millions of years ago. When they died, they fell to the bottom of the lake or seabed, buried under layers of mud and became altered by exposure to high temperature and pressure.

Coal, gas and oil.

A fossil.

This process is called fossilisation.

42

Coal

Coal was formed from plants that grew in swampy areas during the Carboniferous Period, about 300 million years ago. When they died, instead of decaying, they were transformed into peat. The peat was then subjected to high temperatures and pressures over a very long period, and turned into coal.

> Sometimes lumps of coal still have traces of fossil leaves on them.

Problems with fossil fuels

There are three main problems with using fossil fuels to make electricity:

(1) We are using them up much faster than they can form. This means they will eventually run out.

(2) Burning fossil fuels releases a huge amount of carbon dioxide, which is a greenhouse gas and could be contributing to climate change.

(3) Burning fossil fuels releases soot particles and the gas sulphur dioxide, both of which are bad for your lungs, and for buildings. Sulphur dioxide also contributes to acid rain, which damages plants and aquatic animals.

Pollution effects on city buildings.

43

Renewables

If we are running out of fossil fuels, or want to use something less damaging to the environment, we need to find another way to generate electricity in power stations. What we really need are clean sources of energy that won't run out.

These are called renewables. The big problem with some of them is how to store the energy until it's needed. For instance, you can use solar power to generate electricity during daylight, but you have to store it if you want it to power your lights at night.

Sunlight

Solar panels can convert light into DC current. Some buildings now have solar panels on their roofs to supply part of their energy. You can buy solar powered speakers, calculators, toys, phone chargers and many other gadgets. There are even solar powered torches!

Wind power

On hillsides and offshore, you can now see huge wind turbines. The windier it is, the more power they generate, which is why they are built in these places. One problem is that it isn't always windy, so we could never rely on wind power alone for our electricity.

Some people also think the turbines are ugly, and that they are a danger to birds.

Hydropower

Hydropower means using the energy of moving water. Dams can be built across rivers, and the water is then made to flow in a controlled way through turbines, which generate electricity as they turn. People have used moving water as a source of energy for centuries: this was what powered water mills. The first hydroelectric power plant designed by Tesla began to produce electricity in 1881 near Niagara Falls in the USA, and was used to power streetlights in New York City. Hydroelectric power now supplies almost 20% of the world's electricity.

Remember, the greater the height the water falls, the more energy we get.

Wave power

Waves contain enormous amounts of energy, and lots of research is being dedicated to finding ways to harness it. This technology is still at an experimental stage however, and isn't yet being used to generate electricity for general use. One of the problems is that waves are very unpredictable – think of the images you sometimes see of waves crashing over roads and buildings during gales. Tidal power is much more reliable – tides go in and out twice a day, whatever the weather.

Strong waves reaching over the shore.

Other Renewable Fuels

Here are some other ways that we can generate electricity. They all have advantages and disadvantages.

Geothermal energy

This is the process of making use of the heat energy stored in the Earth. There's a huge amount of heat energy down there, but it's difficult to get at it. However, people have been using some geothermal energy for centuries, bathing in hot springs and using the hot water to supply public baths and underfloor heating. It is now being used to generate electricity in a number of countries, with Iceland getting 30% of its electricity this way. This is because in Iceland the high temperatures are present near the surface of the ground, which makes it much easier to use the energy.

Is that my poo?

Biomass

Biomass is simply a word for any animal or plant remains that can be burnt to generate heat energy. This can then be converted to electricity. The most commonly burnt biomass is wood. Other examples are straw and poultry manure.

It also means that the area is often rocked by volcanic eruptions!

Biofuels

Biomass can also be converted into fuels like ethanol and methane. These are called biofuels. Methane is released by all sorts of rotting animal and plant material – and also by belching cows – and is sometimes called biogas. Sadly, it's unlikely you'll ever be able to fill up your car with methane belched into the fuel tank by specially trained cows!

Biodiesel can be made from vegetable oil that has been used for frying food in chip shops and restaurants. There is also lots of research going on into growing algae (basically pond weed) as this can be used to produce a number of biofuels.

Problems with biomass and biofuels

Both of these sound like great ideas, but they have drawbacks. Some edible crops like maize and sugar cane are now being grown specifically to produce bioethanol instead of being used to feed people. Is this really the best use we can make of them?

Oil palms are grown for their oil. At one time it was only used in foods, but is now also used as a source of biodiesel. Huge areas of natural forest in countries like Indonesia and Malaysia have been cut down so that oil palms can be grown instead in huge plantations. This destruction of their habitats has threatened endangered species like the Orang-utan and the Sumatran tiger.

Deforestation in Malaysia, the natural habitat of many endangered species.

47

Transistors

The introduction to this book mentioned some of the modern devices that we all take for granted that use electricity.

Televisions, computers, games consoles, mobile phones, the list goes on and on. These have all been made possible since the accidental discovery of an electronic component, called the transistor, in 1947.

A transistor is an electronic switch. A mechanical switch is one you have to press:

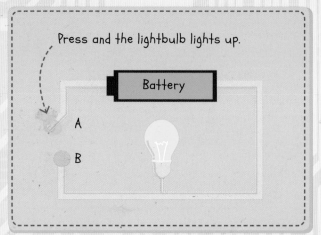

Press and the lightbulb lights up.

Battery

A

B

A transistor does the same job, but you don't need to press it.

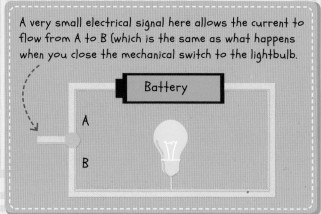

A very small electrical signal here allows the current to flow from A to B (which is the same as what happens when you close the mechanical switch to the lightbulb.

Battery

A

B

The first transistors looked a bit like a baked bean with three legs sticking out (but no tomato sauce). You can still buy transistors like this, but it is more usual now to find them built into integrated circuits. The most recent smartphones have over a billion transistors in them and the most recent computers have as many transistors in one box as there are people on the Earth!

Why do we need so many electronic switches?

Look at a computer screen. The picture is made up of lots of tiny dots called pixels. Each dot can be switched on or off and this is done by at least one transistor for each pixel, and usually more, as the colour of each pixel can be changed from red to green to blue. So, to make a clear moving picture you need lots of dots switching on and off and changing colour very quickly indeed, which takes a huge number of transistors.

Think about that next time you watch a funny cat video on the Internet!

Semi-conductors

The first transistors were made from an element called germanium. After a few years, silicon became more popular for making them, partly because it's so common – it's the most common element on the surface of the Earth. Germanium and silicon are semi-conductors. Semi-conductors are materials that get better at conducting electricity the hotter they become, unlike ordinary conductors – metals – that get worse at conducting electricity the hotter they become.

Silicon chip.

Integrated circuits

By the 1970s scientists were making integrated circuits (these are big circuits made by adding together lots of little ones) with millions of transistors in them on a piece of silicon the size of your little finger nail! This meant it was now possible to make computers small enough to fit in your hand.

Silicon Valley

A lot of the early work on integrated circuits and computers was carried out in a region of California in the USA, which became known as Silicon Valley. Companies like Google, Apple, eBay, Hewlett Packard and Intel are based there or started off there.

Those pesky rechargers...

The problem with semi-conductor integrated circuits and all the products made with them, is that they need a DC power supply. Sometimes this is a battery, but you often need a box of electronics that convert the AC supply in your home to DC in order to recharge these devices. This is why 'chargers' for things like mobile phones are bigger than ordinary plugs.

The Future

It's 200 years since Galvani and Volta discovered electricity but there's still a lot to find out about how we can use electricity. Here are some exciting inventions that are currently being developed. I wonder which one you'll be able to buy and use first?

Superconductors

These are usually very cold materials, which conduct electricity without getting hot. We have known about them since 1911 and they are now used in things like MRI scanners. At CERN lots of research is being carried out to find materials which will 'superconduct' at room temperature.

Artificial intelligence

Researchers are trying to develop computers which generate their own programs and so can make their own decisions. AI has been around in science fiction for a long time, but could it become science fact in the near future?

Robots

These mix some of the earliest electronic devices – motors – with modern ones like computers. They are becoming more sophisticated all the time, and in a few years it's possible that there will be robots, which can help with babysitting and looking after elderly people. The most advanced robot in existence at the moment is called ASIMO. It can walk, run, dance, climb stairs and even serve drinks!

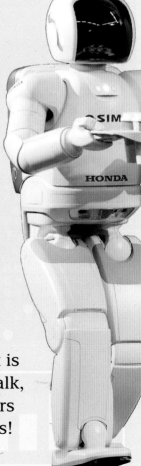

Wearable technology

...or tech togs as they are also known, are pieces of clothing or accessories that incorporate computers and electronics. There are already smartwatches, but how do you fancy a pair of trousers with a keyboard built in? Or a shirt that lights up?

In Dubai, its already possible to take the tube without anyone driving it!

A driverless tube in Dubai.

Driverless cars

There are already electric cars on the roads, but in the next few years, we may see cars that don't need a driver! Several companies have already produced prototype cars with a huge number of electronic sensors and enough computing power to drive themselves safely on public roads. Who knows, one day soon you may be able to read this book in a car that's automatically taking you where you want to go!

Try It Yourself

Trick cling film!

Electrical charges can attract or repel each other. You can easily demonstrate this (and play a trick on someone at the same time!).

If you unroll some cling film, and then roll it back up, it will stick to itself. Unroll a bit of cling film, cut off a thin strip and hang it over the middle finger of one hand (ask an adult to help you with this part). Rub the middle finger of the other hand down the inner surface of the two dangling bits of cling film. Hey presto! The ends of the cling film will now repel each other.

Now you can show it to your parents and tell them they've bought faulty cling film!

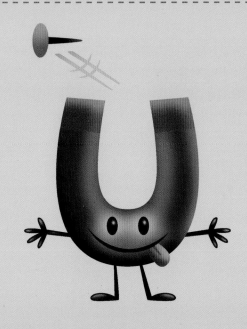

Make a magnet

You can make your own magnet — the only catch is — you need a magnet to do it!

Take a piece of iron — a nail would work well but make sure you ask permission to use it before beginning this experiment. Stroke your magnet along the iron nail in the same direction twenty to thirty times. If it's a horseshoe magnet, only use one end of it.

It's as simple as that! Your iron nail is now magnetised and you have a magnetic nail!

Make a fruit battery

You will need:

Wire (copper is best)

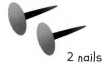
2 nails

2 lemons

Masking tape

A solarpowered calculator

2 penny coins

What to do:

Ask an adult to help you with the following:

1. Take the battery out of the calculator and cover the solar cell with masking tape so no light reaches it.
2. Get an adult to help you cut three pieces of wire about 15 centimetres long.
3. Wrap the end of a wire around one penny.
4. Cut a small slit in one lemon and push the wire-wrapped penny halfway in.
5. Wrap another piece of wire around the second penny in the same way, but wrap the other end of the wire round one of the nails. Cut a slit in the second lemon for the second penny and push the nail into the first lemon.
6. Wrap one end of the final wire round the other nail and push it into the second lemon.
7. If you touch the two free ends of wire to the contacts in the battery compartment of the calculator, it should come on! This can be a bit fiddly but don't give up! The lemon is acting as a battery, and you have built a circuit for the electricity to flow around.

You can find a demonstration of what to do at:

https://www.youtube.com/watch?v=AY9qcDCFeVI

Design an electronic quiz board

You will need:

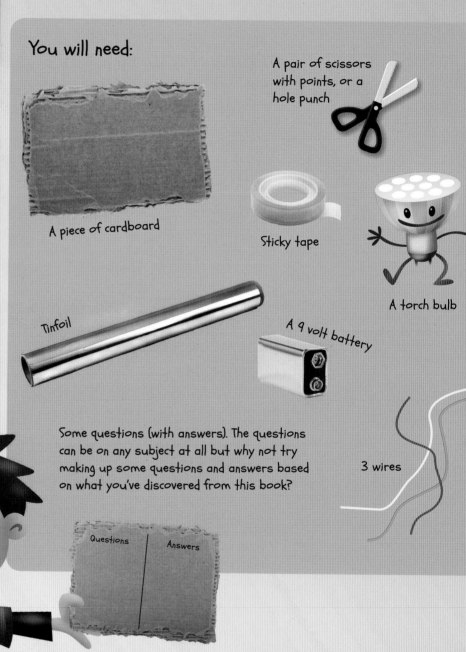

A piece of cardboard

A pair of scissors with points, or a hole punch

Sticky tape

A torch bulb

Tinfoil

A 9 volt battery

Some questions (with answers). The questions can be on any subject at all but why not try making up some questions and answers based on what you've discovered from this book?

3 wires

Questions   Answers

What to do:

1. Draw a line down the middle of the card.

2. Write your questions on one side of the line.

3. Write the answers on the other side of the line — but not so that the question is opposite the correct answer.

4. Get an adult to help you make a hole beside each question and each answer with the scissors or hole punch.

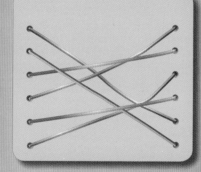

Questions	Answers
Question 1	Answer a
Question 2	Answer b
Question 3	Answer c
Question 4	Answer d
Question 5	Answer e
Question 6	Answer f

5. Cut some thin strips of foil (about one centimetre wide).

6. Turn the card over, and stick a strip of foil down with tape so that it connects the hole beside the first question with the hole beside its correct answer. It's important that the foil is completely covered with tape.

7. Repeat for each question and answer pair.

8. Turn the card over. You should be able to see the foil through each hole.

9. Now connect the wires, bulb and battery as shown.

10. To use the quiz board, press the end of one wire to the foil beside question one, and the other wire to the foil beside the answer.
If you are right, the bulb will light up!

Timeline

Electricity!

1600:
William Gilbert first uses the term 'electricity'.

400 BC:
Democritus proposes the theory that all matter is made of atoms.

1780:
Luigi Galvani discovers that electricity makes muscles twitch.

1820:
Hans Christian Oersted finds that electricity and magnetism are related.

1820:
Andre-Marie Ampere publishes a combined theory of electricity and magnetism.

1878:
Thomas Edison invents an improved lightbulb.

1865:
James Clerk Maxwell works out the maths behind electromagnetism.

1800

0   1600

1747:
Benjamin Franklin discovers there are two types of charge and names them positive and negative.

600 BC:
Thales of Miletus describes what we now call static electricity.

1790:
Alessandro Volta invents the first battery.

1831:
Michael Faraday invents the electric motor.

1882:
Edison switches on the first DC generator supp power to customers

58

Electrons

1897:
J J Thomson
discovers the
electron.

1943:
Tommy Flowers develops
the first electric
programmable computer,
called Colossus.

1957:
Bardeen, Brattain and
Shockley win the
Nobel Prize for
Physics for inventing
the transistor.

1967:
First handheld
calculator
invented by a
team led by
Jack Kilby.

1973:
First mobile phone
released by Motorola.

2014:
Isamu Akasaki, Hiroshi
Amano and Shuji Nakamura
are awarded Nobel Prize
for Physics for creating
blue light LED.

2000

1900

1947:
John Bardeen, Walter
Brattain and William
Shockley invent
the transistor.

1972:
First home video
games are
introduced.

1978:
Space Invaders
game is launched.

1958:
Jack Kilby invents the
integrated circuit.

Find Out More

Visit

The Science Museum in London to see the new Information Age Gallery.
http://www.sciencemuseum.org.uk

The Lancaster Science Factory to see their electricity and magnetism exhibits.
http://www.lancastersciencefactory.org

The Cambridge Science Centre for lots of exhibits on electricity and magnetism.
http://www.cambridgesciencecentre.org

Read

Answer by Fredric Brown (Originally appeared in Angles and Spaceships 1954)
A short science fiction story which looks at what happens if you ask an intelligent computer the question 'Is there a God?'

A Beginner's Guide to the Periodic Table by Gill Arbuthnott (A & C Black, 2014)
A brilliant guide to the periodic table.

Log on to

http://www.youtube.com/watch?v=Ux-QGhbjOA0
To find instructions on how to make a simple electric motor.

http://www.youtube.com/watch?v=skXYr8BzjpM
To see just what the ASIMO robot can do, and prepare to be amazed!

Remember to always ask permission before logging on to the videos above.

Glossary

Alloy Metal made of a mix of two or more different metals

Amp (Ampere) Unit used to measure electric current

Atom The smallest part of an element; a building block from which everything is made up

Bifocal Glasses with lenses divided into two parts, one for looking at things far away and one for looking at things that are near

Capacitor Device that can store electrical energy

Circuit Closed path that an electric current can follow

Concept Idea or thought

Contracted Got shorter when tensing up

Core Innermost part

Cosmic Of the whole universe

Cumulonimbus Thunderstorm clouds

Dedicated Totally committed to

DNA Material that carries all the information needed for a living thing to develop

Electric chair Method of killing a criminal by strapping them to a chair and electrocuting them

Electron Small particle within an atom that has a negative charge

Element A pure substance that contains a single type of atom

Emits Gives out

Exposure Being unprotected, left open

Fluorescent Gives out visible light when exposed to invisible ultra-violet light

Fossil fuel Fuel (oil, gas or coal) formed from the remains of dead plants and animals

Generator Device that changes mechanical energy into electrical energy

Greenhouse gas Gas (such as carbon dioxide) that traps the sun's heat in the atmosphere, making the Earth too warm

Higgs Boson A type of particle

Incandescent Giving out light when heated

Inert Inactive (will not react with another chemical)

Lodestone Natural magnetic iron ore (mineral)

Magnetoreception A sense in some animals that allows them to detect magnetic fields

Molten Made into a liquid by heating

Neutron Small particle within an atom that has no charge

Nuclear power Energy released by splitting atoms

Nucleus Centre of an atom

Ore Mineral that contains metal

Pacemaker Small electrical machine put inside someone to make their heart beat evenly

Philosopher Someone who studies ideas about the meaning of life

Pixels Tiny dots that make up the picture on a computer or television screen

Preserved Kept in original state

Proton Small particle within an atom that has a positive charge

Prototype An early model that later models will be based on and developed from

Radiation Energy released from something. Many types of radiation are dangerous

Radioactive Releasing a type of energy called radiation

Repel Force to move apart

Rotation Complete turn around a central point

Solar From the sun

Static electricity Electricity that builds up in one place, rather than flowing as a current

Temperamental Unpredictable

Toxic Poisonous

Transformer Device that increases or decreases the voltage of electrical energy

Transistor Electronic switch

Tungsten Metal used to make the wire in lightbulbs

Turbine Type of water wheel made to move by the pressure of water or steam

Vaporised Made into vapour (small drops of liquid mixed with air)

Volt Unit of measurement in electricity

Index

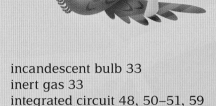